Louis Moyse Flute Collection

Sixty-five Little Pieces
In Progressive Order for Beginner Flutists

Transcribed and Adapted
for Flute and Piano by
Louis Moyse

ED-3741

ISBN 978-0-7935-4814-9

G. SCHIRMER, Inc.

DISTRIBUTED BY

 **HAL•LEONARD®**
CORPORATION

7777 W. BLUEMOUND RD. P.O. BOX 13819 MILWAUKEE, WI 53213

CONTENTS

Sixty-Five Little Pieces
for Flute and Piano

1
Novelette

ROBERT SCHUMANN
Edited by Louis Moyse

2
Consolation

FRANZ LISZT
Edited by Louis Moyse

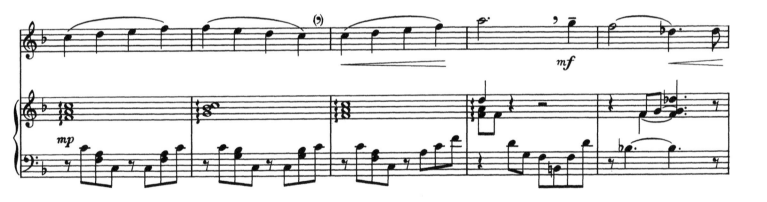

3
Menuetto

GEORGE FREDERICK HANDEL
Edited by Louis Moyse

4
Chanson Triste

PETER ILYICH TCHAIKOVSKY
Edited by Louis Moyse

5
Menuetto

LUDWIG van BEETHOVEN
Edited by Louis Moyse

Poco allegretto

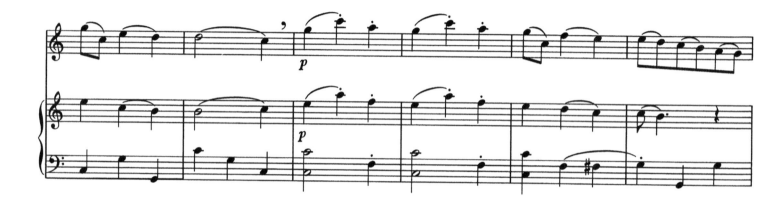

6
From: Piano Sonata

EDVARD GRIEG
Edited by Louis Moyse

7
The Smooth Tongued

FRANÇOIS COUPERIN
Edited by Louis Moyse

Gracefully

8
Song

FELIX MENDELSSOHN
Edited by Louis Moyse

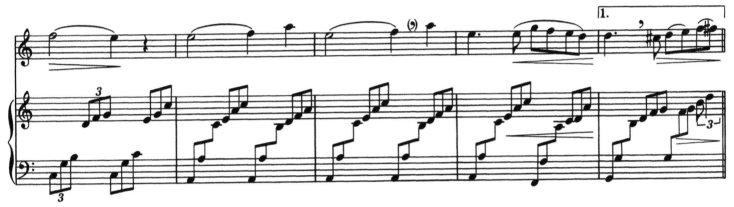

9
Ballade

FRÉDÉRIC CHOPIN
Edited by Louis Moyse

Andantino

10
Theme from "La Molinara"
(Paisiello)

LUDWIG VAN BEETHOVEN
Edited by Louis Moyse

11
Andante

ANTONIO VIVALDI
Edited by Louis Moyse

Cantabile

12
Aria from Piano Sonata

FRANZ SCHUBERT
Edited by Louis Moyse

13
Menuetto

WOLFGANG AMADEUS MOZART
Edited by Louis Moyse

14
Waltz

JOHANNES BRAHMS
Edited by Louis Moyse

Poco lento

15
A Gondolier Song

FELIX MENDELSSOHN
Edited by Louis Moyse

16
Siciliana

GEORGE FREDERICK HANDEL
Edited by Louis Moyse

17
Impromptu

FRANZ SCHUBERT
Edited by Louis Moyse

Allegretto

18
Lied

ROBERT SCHUMANN
Edited by Louis Moyse

19
Menuetto

JOSEF HAYDN
Edited by Louis Moyse

Poco lento

20
Aria

Edited by Louis Moyse

Andante

21
To Spring

EDVARD GRIEG
Edited by Louis Moyse

22
Prelude

FRÉDÉRIC CHOPIN
Edited by Louis Moyse

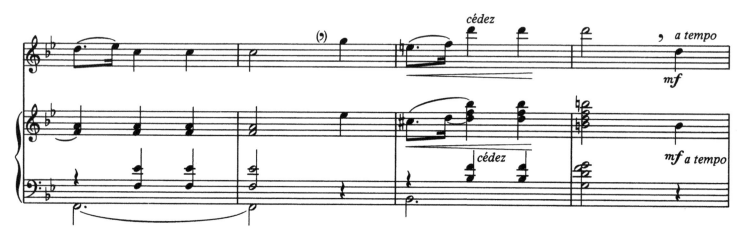

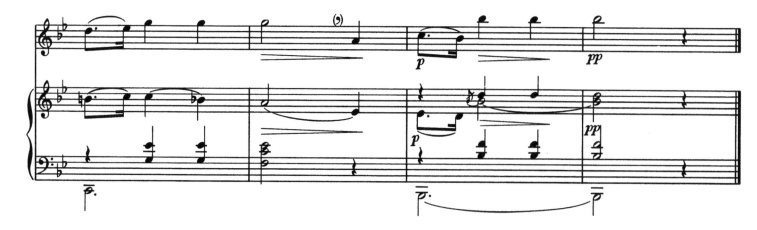

23
Song

FELIX MENDELSSOHN
Edited by Louis Moyse

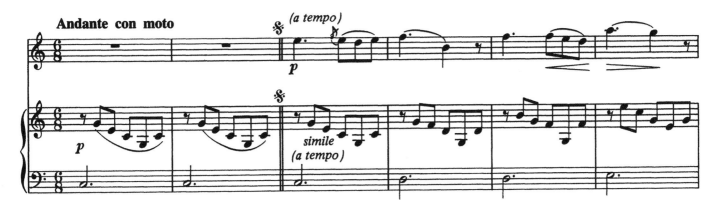

24
Sarabande

GEORGE FREDERICK HANDEL
Edited by Louis Moyse

25
Rondo

LUDWIG ᴠᴀɴ BEETHOVEN
Edited by Louis Moyse

26
Fantasia

WOLFGANG AMADEUS MOZART
Edited by Louis Moyse

Allegretto

27
Spring Dance

EDVARD GRIEG
Edited by Louis Moyse

Allegretto marcato

28
Sister Monique

FRANÇOIS COUPERIN
Edited by Louis Moyse

29
Finale

JOSEF HAYDN
Edited by Louis Moyse

Presto ma non troppo

30
Sarabande

LOUIS MOYSE

31
Andante Consolante

CARL MARIA von WEBER
Edited by Louis Moyse

Quasi allegretto

32
Tambourin

JEAN PHILIPPE RAMEAU
Edited by Louis Moyse

33
Theme

LUDWIG van BEETHOVEN
Edited by Louis Moyse

Andante quasi
Allegretto

34
Prelude

FRÉDÉRIC CHOPIN
Edited by Louis Moyse

Sostenuto

Flute part

Sixty-five Little Pieces

In Progressive Order for Beginner Flutists

Transcribed and Adapted
for Flute and Piano by
Louis Moyse

ED-3741

ISBN 978-0-7935-4814-9

G. SCHIRMER, Inc.

DISTRIBUTED BY

HAL•LEONARD®
CORPORATION
7777 W. BLUEMOUND RD. P.O. BOX 13819 MILWAUKEE, WI 53213

CONTENTS

Sixty-Five Little Pieces
for Flute and Piano

Flute

1
Novelette

ROBERT SCHUMANN
Edited by Louis Moyse

2
Consolation

FRANZ LISZT
Edited by Louis Moyse

3
Menuetto

GEORGE FREDERICK HANDEL
Edited by Louis Moyse

4
Chanson Triste

PETER ILYICH TCHAIKOVSKY
Edited by Louis Moyse

5
Menuetto

LUDWIG van BEETHOVEN
Edited by Louis Moyse

6
From: Piano Sonata

EDVARD GRIEG
Edited by Louis Moyse

7
The Smooth Tongued

FRANCOIS COUPERIN
Edited by Louis Moyse

8
Song

FELIX MENDELSSOHN
Edited by Louis Moyse

9
Ballade

FRÉDÉRIC CHOPIN
Edited by Louis Moyse

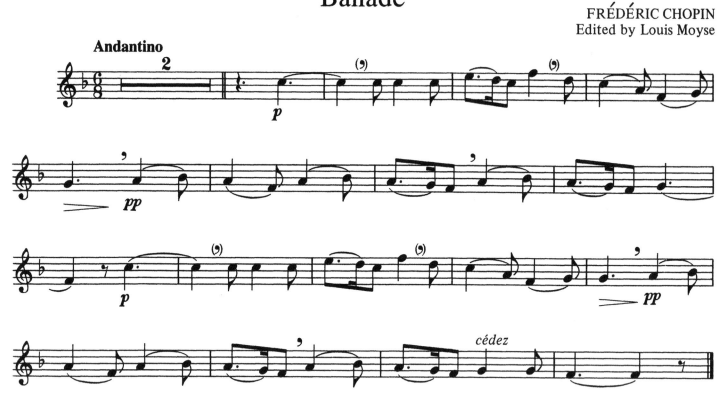

10
Theme from "La Molinara"
(Paisiello)

LUDWIG VAN BEETHOVEN
Edited by Louis Moyse

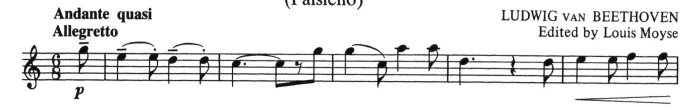

11
Andante

ANTONIO VIVALDI
Edited by Louis Moyse

12
Aria from Piano Sonata

FRANZ SCHUBERT
Edited by Louis Moyse

13
Menuetto

WOLFGANG AMADEUS MOZART
Edited by Louis Moyse

14
Waltz

JOHANNES BRAHMS
Edited by Louis Moyse

15
A Gondolier Song

FELIX MENDELSSOHN
Edited by Louis Moyse

Allegretto tranquillo

16
Siciliana

GEORGE FREDERICK HANDEL
Edited by Louis Moyse

Andantino

17
Impromptu

FRANZ SCHUBERT
Edited by Louis Moyse

18
Lied

ROBERT SCHUMANN
Edited by Louis Moyse

19
Menuetto

JOSEF HAYDN
Edited by Louis Moyse

20
Aria

WOLFGANG AMADEUS MOZART
Edited by Louis Moyse

21
To Spring

EDVARD GRIEG
Edited by Louis Moyse

22
Prelude

FRÉDÉRIC CHOPIN
Edited by Louis Moyse

23
Song

FELIX MENDELSSOHN
Edited by Louis Moyse

24
Sarabande

GEORGE FREDERICK HANDEL
Edited by Louis Moyse

25
Rondo

LUDWIG van BEETHOVEN
Edited by Louis Moyse

26
Fantasia

WOLFGANG AMADEUS MOZART
Edited by Louis Moyse

27
Spring Dance

EDVARD GRIEG
Edited by Louis Moyse

28
Sister Monique

FRANÇOIS COUPERIN
Edited by Louis Moyse

29
Finale

JOSEF HAYDN
Edited by Louis Moyse

30
Sarabande

LOUIS MOYSE

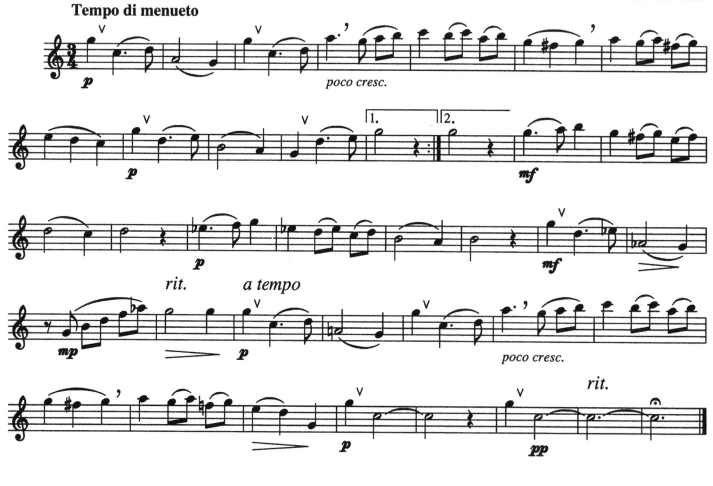

31
Andante Consolante

CARL MARIA von WEBER
Edited by Louis Moyse

32
Tambourin

JEAN PHILIPPE RAMEAU
Edited by Louis Moyse

33
Theme

LUDWIG van BEETHOVEN
Edited by Louis Moyse

34
Prelude

FRÉDÉRIC CHOPIN
Edited by Louis Moyse

35
Sarabande

JOHANN SEBASTIAN BACH
Edited by Louis Moyse

36
Gavotte

GEORGE FREDERICK HANDEL
Edited by Louis Moyse

37
Andante

CARL MARIA von WEBER
Edited by Louis Moyse

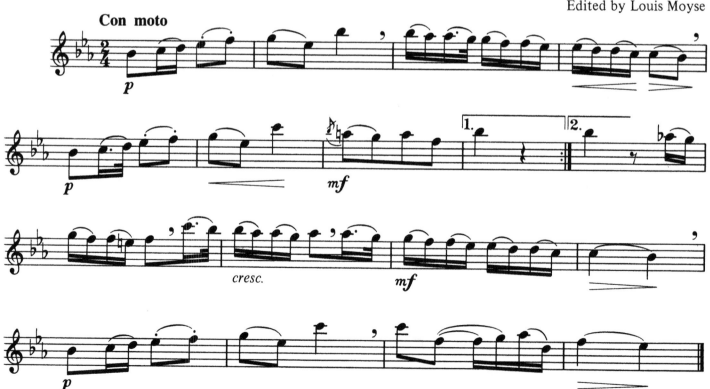

38
Happy Farmer

ROBERT SCHUMANN
Edited by Louis Moyse

39
Pièce de Concert

FRANZ SCHUBERT
Edited by Louis Moyse

40
Caprice

FELIX MENDELSSOHN
Edited by Louis Moyse

41
Tender Nanette

FRANÇOIS COUPERIN
Edited by Louis Moyse

42
Bourrée

JOHANN SEBASTIAN BACH
Edited by Louis Moyse

Allegro

43
Adagio

JOSEF HAYDN
Edited by Louis Moyse

Poco lento

cresc.   p   3   3

cresc.   mf   3   3   mf

cédez   a tempo

mp   pp

3

mp   p   pp

44
Aria

WOLFGANG AMADEUS MOZART
Edited by Louis Moyse

Larghetto cantabile

1. mp
2. pp   2. p

1.   2.

pp   mp

1.   2.

p

mp

45
Bagatelle

LUDWIG van BEETHOVEN
Edited by Louis Moyse

46
Theme

FELIX MENDELSSOHN
Edited by Louis Moyse

47
Funny Story

ROBERT SCHUMANN
Edited by Louis Moyse

48
Nocturne

FRÉDÉRIC CHOPIN
Edited by Louis Moyse

49
Dance

GEORGE FREDERICK HANDEL
Edited by Louis Moyse

50
Menuetto

JOSEF HAYDN
Edited by Louis Moyse

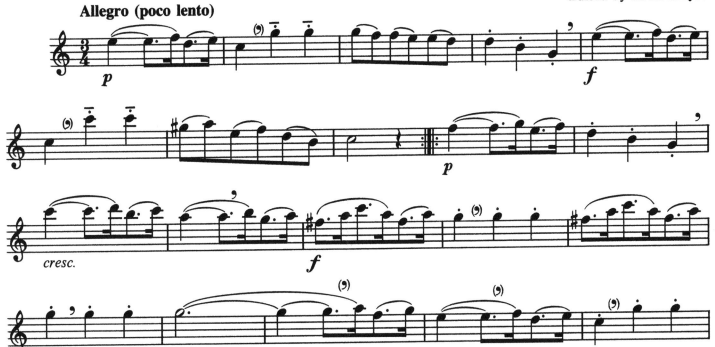

51
Rustic Dance

FRANZ SCHUBERT
Edited by Louis Moyse

52
Gavotte

JOHANN SEBASTIAN BACH
Edited by Louis Moyse

53
Waltz

CARL MARIA von WEBER
Edited by Louis Moyse

54
Folk Song

ROBERT SCHUMANN
Edited by Louis Moyse

55
Rondo

WOLFGANG AMADEUS MOZART
Edited by Louis Moyse

Andante

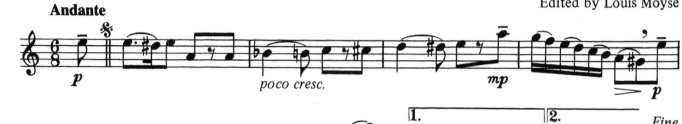

56
Sarabande

CLAUDE DEBUSSY
Edited by Louis Moyse

Grave et lent

57
Morning Mood

EDVARD GRIEG
Edited by Louis Moyse

58
Menuetto

JOHANN SEBASTIAN BACH
Edited by Louis Moyse

59
Fantasie Impromptu

FRÉDÉRIC CHOPIN
Edited by Louis Moyse

60
Solvejg's Song

EDVARD GRIEG
Edited by Louis Moyse

61
The Girl with the Flaxen Hair

CLAUDE DEBUSSY
Edited by Louis Moyse

62
Song

FRANZ SCHUBERT
Edited by Louis Moyse

63
Polonaise

JOHANN SEBASTIAN BACH
Edited by Louis Moyse

64
Rondo

JOSEF HAYDN
Edited by Louis Moyse

65
Dialogue

G.P. TELEMANN
Edited by Louis Moyse

35
Sarabande

JOHANN SEBASTIAN BACH
Edited by Louis Moyse

Andante con moto

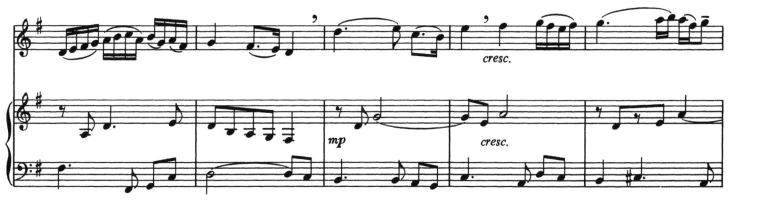

36
Gavotte

GEORGE FREDERICK HANDEL
Edited by Louis Moyse

37
Andante

CARL MARIA von WEBER
Edited by Louis Moyse

38
Happy Farmer

ROBERT SCHUMANN
Edited by Louis Moyse

39
Pièce de Concert

FRANZ SCHUBERT
Edited by Louis Moyse

40
Caprice

FELIX MENDELSSOHN
Edited by Louis Moyse

41
Tender Nanette

FRANÇOIS COUPERIN
Edited by Louis Moyse

42
Bourrée

JOHANN SEBASTIAN BACH
Edited by Louis Moyse

43
Adagio

JOSEF HAYDN
Edited by Louis Moyse

44
Aria

WOLFGANG AMADEUS MOZART
Edited by Louis Moyse

Larghetto cantabile

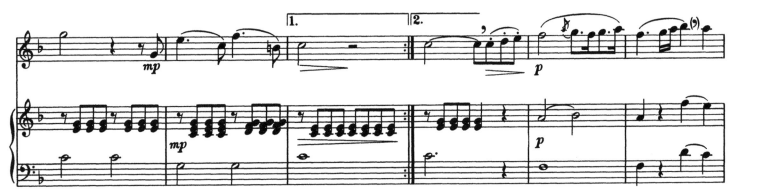

45
Bagatelle

LUDWIG van BEETHOVEN
Edited by Louis Moyse

46
Theme

FELIX MENDELSSOHN
Edited by Louis Moyse

Andante

47
Funny Story

ROBERT SCHUMANN
Edited by Louis Moyse

Tempo di mazurka

48
Nocturne

FRÉDÉRIC CHOPIN
Edited by Louis Moyse

Andante

(continued on page 58)

49
Dance

GEORGE FREDERICK HANDEL
Edited by Louis Moyse

50
Menuetto

JOSEF HAYDN
Edited by Louis Moyse

Allegro (poco lento)

51
Rustic Dance

FRANZ SCHUBERT
Edited by Louis Moyse

Allegretto

52
Gavotte

JOHANN SEBASTIAN BACH
Edited by Louis Moyse

53
Waltz

CARL MARIA VON WEBER
Edited by Louis Moyse

54
Folk Song

ROBERT SCHUMANN
Edited by Louis Moyse

55
Rondo

WOLFGANG AMADEUS MOZART
Edited by Louis Moyse

56
Sarabande

CLAUDE DEBUSSY
Edited by Louis Moyse

Grave et lent

57
Morning Mood

EDVARD GRIEG
Edited by Louis Moyse

Allegretto pastorale
(a tempo)

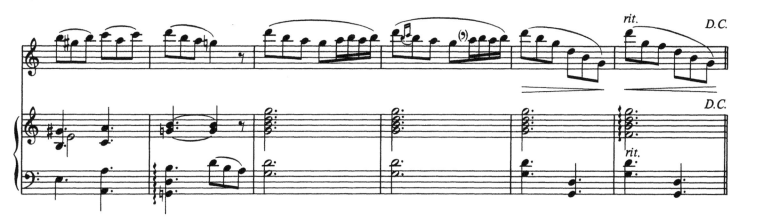

58
Menuetto

JOHANN SEBASTIAN BACH
Edited by Louis Moyse

Poco allegretto

59
Fantasie Impromptu

FRÉDÉRIC CHOPIN
Edited by Louis Moyse

Moderato cantabile

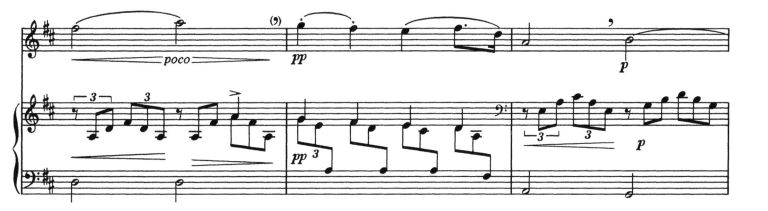

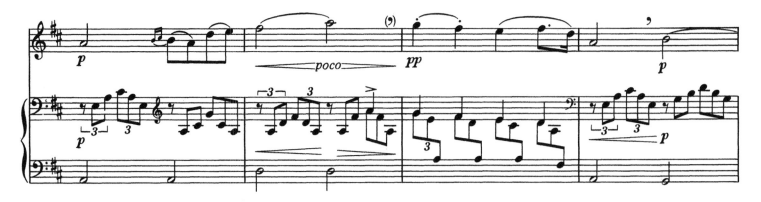

60
Solvejg's Song

EDVARD GRIEG
Edited by Louis Moyse

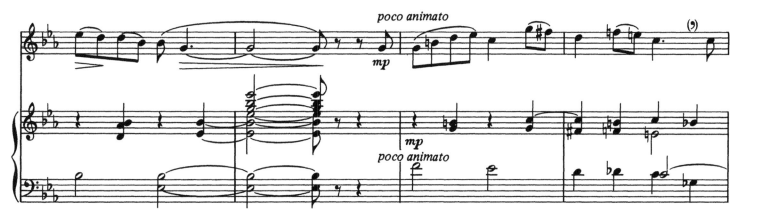

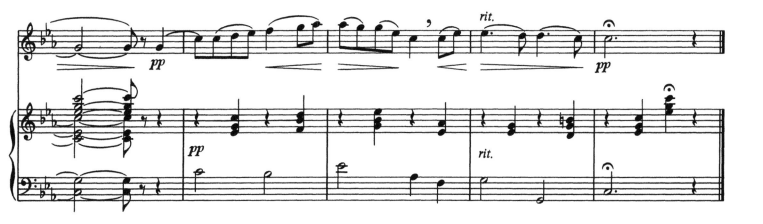

61
The Girl with the Flaxen Hair

CLAUDE DEBUSSY
Edited by Louis Moyse

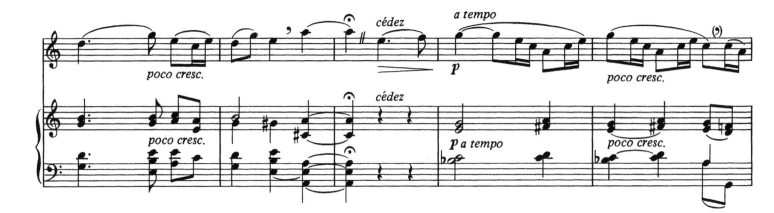

62
Song

FRANZ SCHUBERT
Edited by Louis Moyse

Allegro moderato

63
Polonaise

JOHANN SEBASTIAN BACH
Edited by Louis Moyse

64
Rondo

JOSEF HAYDN
Edited by Louis Moyse

Allegro

(continued on page 76)

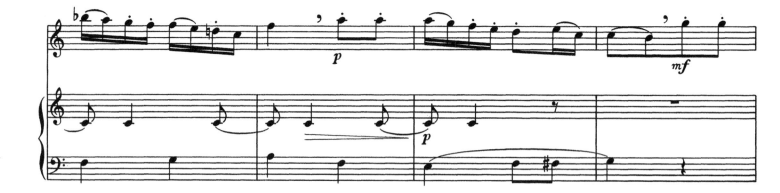

65
Dialogue

G.P. TELEMANN
Edited by Louis Moyse

Soave (Andante)